I0814282

MINING IN AMERICA

MINING TECHNIQUES

BY BONNIE HINMAN

Core Library
An Imprint of Abdo Publishing
abdobooks.com

Cover image: Large mining equipment such as excavators and haul trucks are used in mines today.

abdobooks.com

Published by Abdo Publishing, a division of ABDO, PO Box 398166, Minneapolis, Minnesota 55439.

Printed in the United States of America, North Mankato, Minnesota.
052023
092023

Cover Photo: iStockphoto
Interior Photos: Michael Lynch/EyeEm/Getty Images, 4–5; iStockphoto, 7; John Greim/LightRocket/Getty Images, 10–11; John Flavell/AP Images, 13; Shutterstock Images, 14, 43; Red Line Editorial, 16, 30; Erik Von Weber/The Image Bank/Getty Images, 18; Benjamin Lowy/Getty Images News/Getty Images, 20–21, 45; David Goldman/AP Images, 23; John Schultz/Quad-City Times/ZUMA Wire/Alamy, 25; Matt Joyce/AP Images, 27; Carolyn Cole/Los Angeles Times/Getty Images, 32–33; Jeff Greenberg/Universal Images Group/Getty Images, 35; John Cancalosi/Alamy, 38; Victor Habbick Visions/Science Source, 40

Editor: Angela Lim
Series Designer: Ryan Gale

Library of Congress Control Number: 2022949132

Publisher's Cataloging-in-Publication Data
Names: Hinman, Bonnie, author.
Title: Mining Techniques / by Bonnie Hinman
Description: Minneapolis, Minnesota: Abdo Publishing Company, 2024 | Series: Mining in America | Includes online resources and index.
Identifiers: ISBN 9781098290986 (lib. bdg.) | ISBN 9781098277161 (ebook)
Subjects: LCSH: Mines and mining--Juvenile literature. | Mines and mineral resources--Juvenile literature. | Mining engineering--Juvenile literature. | United States--Juvenile literature.
Classification: DDC 622.0973--dc23

CONTENTS

CHAPTER ONE

BLAST ZONE

Thousands of miners are hard at work at the Bingham Canyon mine in Utah. They are mining copper, a metal that is used in construction, electronics, and more. The Bingham Canyon mine is an open-pit mine. It is a deep hole that is wider at the top than it is at the bottom. It is divided into layers called terraces, where mining occurs.

One worker drives a drill rig. She uses the large machine to drill holes into a terrace.

The Bingham Canyon mine produces more than 16 percent of the copper mined in the United States.

Another worker places explosives in the holes. The workers back away from the explosives. When they are a safe distance away, the second worker presses a button on a device. The explosives go off, and the rock around the holes crumbles. A huge cloud of dust rises in the air.

The loose rock contains copper ore. Ore is a rock that contains metals or minerals. These materials need to be separated from the rock before they can be used. Machines called loaders move the rocks onto haul trucks. After the truck is fully loaded, a worker drives

THE BINGHAM CANYON MINE

The Bingham Canyon mine opened in 1906. Since then it has become the deepest open-pit mine in the world. It is nearly 0.75 miles (1.2 km) deep and almost 2.5 miles (4 km) wide. The Bingham Canyon mine is also called the Kennecott Copper Mine because copper is the primary material extracted from the mine. In 2018 the mine produced approximately 335,000 tons (303,900 metric tons) of copper. It also produces gold, silver, and a mineral called molybdenum.

Mining surveyors use special equipment to locate mineral deposits.

the truck to the top of the mine. He dumps the rocks onto a long conveyor belt that transports the copper ore to a processing plant.

WHAT IS MINING?

Mining is the process of extracting, or removing, useful materials from the ground. The first step in opening a new mine is to locate mineral deposits. Sometimes a mineral-rich area is already known. Other times a mining company employs a mineral explorer to find new deposits. Mineral explorers may use planes or helicopters to look for the rock formations that are likely to have mineral deposits. Mineral explorers take pictures, make maps, and measure the magnetism of the ground. Some mined materials are magnetic. A high level of magnetism may indicate a deposit. Mineral explorers also take samples of rocks, soil, and water. The chemicals found in these samples can show if there are valuable minerals present.

After locating a large deposit, mining companies employ mine planners. These workers

PERSPECTIVES

MINING AND RENEWABLE ENERGY

In 2017 more than 90 percent of toxic emissions in Utah came from the Bingham Canyon mine. However, mined materials are necessary to develop products for renewable energy, which will reduce overall emissions in the United States. Ken Ivory served in the Utah House of Representatives in 2022. He defended copper mines, saying, "If you like renewable energy, you should love mining. . . . To do the renewable energy we are seeing and hearing about takes 23 [times more] copper [than is currently produced]."

determine whether the mine will be profitable. They study information about the deposit. A deposit located far underground will be more expensive to mine. And a small deposit may not be worth the expense of developing a mine.

After mineral deposits are located and assessed, a mining company may begin to build a new mine. This process can take years. Modern mines use many mining techniques. Three major methods are surface mining, underground mining, and underwater mining. Each method can involve a variety of techniques that help the mine be successful.

EXPLORE ONLINE

Chapter One describes how new mines are developed. The following website has additional information about this process. Does it answer any questions you have about the development of new mines?

THE MINING CYCLE

abdocorelibrary.com/mining-techniques

CHAPTER TWO

SURFACE MINING

Surface mining is used when a mineral or coal deposit is near the surface of the ground. This mining method is used for about 85 percent of all mining in the United States. It is cheaper than underground mining because it does not use tunnels or shafts that require electricity, water pipes, and support structures. Surface mining is also safer. There is less risk of the mine collapsing on top of workers.

Granite is a light-colored rock that can be mined in surface mines. The Smith Quarry in Vermont is the deepest granite mine in the world.

BLOWING UP ROCKS

Removing minerals and ores from rock typically requires explosives. The first explosive used for mining was black powder. However, this explosive can ignite gases and dust in a coal mine. Deadly explosions can occur. Other explosives were developed. Dynamite was less likely to blow up unexpectedly. Dynamite is still used today, but most mines use ammonium nitrate and fuel oil (ANFO). ANFO is as powerful as dynamite, but it is cheaper and even less likely to blow up at the wrong time.

The first step in surface mining is to remove soil and rocks to access the deposits. The removed soil and rocks are called the overburden. Explosives are often used to break up the ground above deposits. The deposits may include pure minerals, ores, or coal.

Once the overburden is cleared, the deposits can be extracted. Dozers, excavators, and other large earth-moving equipment load the raw materials onto haul trucks. The trucks transport the materials to rock crushers and processing machinery. These machines may be located on-site.

Surface mining techniques, such as mountaintop removal, can damage the environment. For this reason, some people think that new mines should not be developed.

Other times, haul trucks need to transport materials to a separate location to be processed.

Mining companies determine what technique to use for a mine. Surface mining techniques include open-pit, strip, mountaintop removal, and highwall. Mining companies choose the technique that is the most profitable for each deposit.

SURFACE MINING TECHNIQUES

Open-pit mining is used when the ore deposit is located near the surface. The deposit usually covers a

Strong explosives are needed to access ore in open-pit mines.

large area. Overburden is removed, creating a large, open pit from which materials can be extracted. Miners place explosives to expose the ore. Once the ore is exposed, it can be removed quickly. Open-pit mines become deeper and wider over time. Materials may continue to be excavated from an open-pit mine until the deposit runs out. Open-pit mines may also become inactive when it becomes too expensive to remove overburden.

Strip mining is another surface mining technique. It is used most often to mine level deposits of coal that lie just beneath the surface. Strip mining does not create deep pits like open-pit mining does. Machines called stripping shovels clear overburden in long trenches. Coal is excavated from the trenches. As new trenches are being cleared, the overburden is used to fill old trenches that have already been mined.

Mountaintop removal is another surface mining technique used mostly to mine coal. It is common in the Appalachian Mountains. The top of a mountain is cleared of plants and trees. Explosives are used to blast away the dirt for hundreds of meters across the top of the mountain. This exposes the coal underneath. The overburden from the blasting is dumped into nearby valleys. Mountaintop removal became popular in the 1990s. It is cheaper than some other mining techniques. Mountaintop mines also require fewer workers than

COAL PRODUCTION IN THE UNITED STATES, 2011–2021

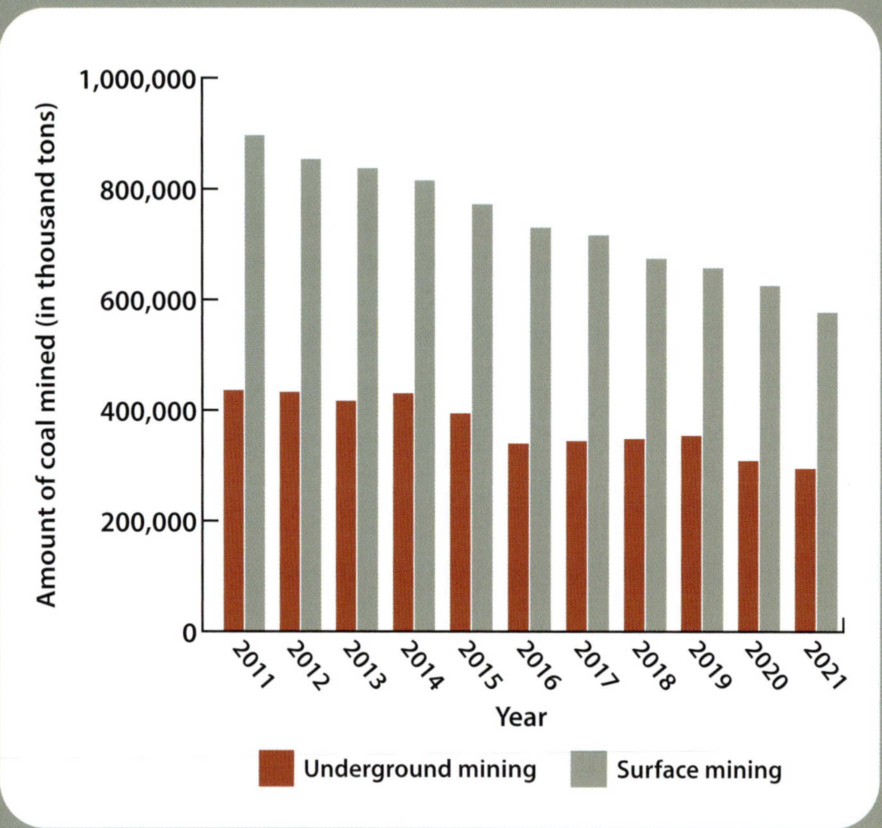

Coal is mined in underground mines and surface mines in the United States. Compare the amount of coal mined in the United States each year from 2011 to 2021. What trend do you notice?

underground mines. Additionally, mountaintop removal exposes large deposits of coal. These mines can be very productive.

HIGHWALL MINING

Open-pit mining, strip mining, and mountaintop removal are most effective when deposits are level and located close to the surface. But some deposits extend deep underground. In these cases, highwall mining can be used.

Highwall mining is often used to access more materials in open-pit mines. These materials may be located in the walls of the mine. There is a lot

PERSPECTIVES

IN-SITU MINING

A liquid solution is pumped underground in in-situ mining. This solution dissolves the material to be mined. The material can then be pumped to the surface. In-situ mining is commonly used to mine uranium. This material can be used as an energy source. But high levels of exposure can harm health. Some people do not think in-situ uranium mines are safe. In 2022 people talked about overturning a Virginia law that bans mining uranium. Vic Ingram was the chairman of a county board in the state. He was in favor of keeping the law in place. He said, "I know the importance of having energy such as uranium. But how much of your community do you sacrifice for this to happen?"

Open-pit mining is the most commonly used surface mining technique.

of overburden covering the deposit. It is too expensive to remove this overburden. Highwall mining machines are driven to the wall where the deposit is located. These machines cut holes into the wall and extract materials. Overburden does not need to be removed. There may be multiple highwall mining sites within an open-pit mine.

Though highwall mining machines tunnel belowground, the machine operators do not go underground themselves. Operators sit in control cabs located at the back of the highwall mining machine. Because the workers do not need to go underground, highwall mining is safer than underground mining.

STRAIGHT TO THE SOURCE

Judy Bonds campaigned to stop mountaintop removal. She came from a coal mining family in Marfork, West Virginia. In a 2009 interview, Bonds talked about why she became an activist:

> *I became an activist because of the fish I witnessed with my grandson in Marfork when he was six years old. One day we found ourselves standing in a river full of dead fish. . . . We noticed black water spills happening almost on a weekly basis. I found out it was coming from the [coal mining dam] just above. It wasn't just affecting us, but this was poisoning the whole town of Whitesville right below us. I know the chemicals and the heavy metals coming from this coal waste have made a lot of local people sick. . . . These people have brain tumors. They have kidney and liver cancer. These people are dying from coal sludge.*

Source: Taylor Lee Kirkland. "Born Fighting: An Interview with Judy Bonds." *Institute for Southern Studies*, Oct. 2009, facingsouth.org. Accessed 12 Oct. 2022.

BACK IT UP

Judy Bonds talked about the effect coal mining had on her community. Write a paragraph describing the point she is making. Then write down two or three pieces of evidence she uses to make the point.

CHAPTER THREE

UNDERGROUND MINING

Underground mining is used when ore deposits are too deep or slanted to easily access from the surface. Underground mines can be dug at the base of a hill or mountain. Other underground mines require vertical shafts that are used to bring materials to the surface. These shafts extend underground until they are level with the deposit. Tunnels are dug, which allow miners to move underground. The tunnels are

The Wellmore coal mine is an underground coal mine in Appalachia. Approximately 82 percent of the coal produced in this region comes from underground mines.

MINING SAFETY

Working in an underground mine can be dangerous. Breathing in mining dust can damage the lungs. Loud noises can harm hearing. Miners are also at risk of becoming trapped in underground mines. The Mine Act is a US law that protects the safety of miners. Mining companies are required to have trained rescue workers in case of an underground emergency. Mine rescue contests are held as part of the training. Team members practice responding to mining disasters as quickly and efficiently as possible.

also where materials from the deposit are excavated.

Workers and machinery are located below the surface in underground mines. These mines are at risk of collapse. They are more dangerous than surface mines. In addition, underground mines require more workers and have more safety measures. Underground mining techniques are expensive because of these requirements.

A mining company has to consider several things before deciding whether to build an underground mine.

Underground miners may need to work in dark, cramped conditions.

The company makes sure the deposit is large enough to be profitable. It takes more time and money to access a deposit that is deep underground. The mining company also checks that it is safe to develop a mine. The rock surrounding the deposit must be strong so that it will not collapse.

The mining company may decide to proceed with the mine after assessing the deposit. It buys an area of property. The mine includes conveyor belts and shafts to bring mined materials to the surface. The mining company also establishes a communication network and escape routes to keep miners safe.

ROOM AND PILLAR MINING

Room and pillar mining is a common underground mining technique in the United States. It is used to mine deposits that are level and deep underground. The deposit is accessed through a system of shafts and tunnels. Blasting is done to loosen the rock. Machines, such as continuous miner machines, are used to excavate ore. The ore is first removed in parallel strips. This creates a line of tunnels that are separated from each other by walls.

Next, the continuous miners begin to remove parts of the walls. But some of the wall remains as pillars that support the overburden. The underground mine begins to take on a grid pattern. It contains excavated rooms and pillars that prevent collapse.

Mining companies use other techniques to maximize ore extraction in room and pillar mines. The room and pillar mining technique cannot extract all the ore in the mine. Some of the ore remains in the pillars. When room and pillar mining stops producing ore,

The size of pillars depends on the weight of overburden and strength of the rock.

mining companies may begin to use retreat mining. This form of mining begins farthest from the mine's entrance. Miners use machinery to remove the support pillars and extract the ore. They also need machinery to support the overburden and keep them safe from collapse. Retreat mining continues until all the pillars are removed.

LONGWALL MINING

Longwall mining is used to excavate long, horizontal deposits that are deep underground. Deposits may be hundreds of feet long. This technique usually supplements room and pillar mining and is often used to mine coal. The rooms in these mines expose coal in the walls. Machines can then run along the face of the wall to remove the coal.

A longwall mining machine has several key features. It has a plow or shear that cuts into the wall. The machine is also equipped with a conveyor belt. As materials are cut from the wall, they fall onto the conveyor belt. The conveyor belt moves the material to a crusher, which breaks up the material into small pieces that can be taken to the surface. A longwall mining machine also has strong roof supports. Though miners do not have to remove materials from the walls themselves, they must stand nearby to supervise the process. The roof supports offer protection from overburden collapse.

A mine business analyst watches as a longwall mining machine removes a mineral called trona from the wall of an underground mine.

OTHER UNDERGROUND MINING TECHNIQUES

Certain conditions can make room and pillar mining less effective. The deposit may be slanted at an angle rather than horizontal. The rock surrounding the deposit may be weak. In these cases, other underground mining techniques are used.

Shrinkage stope mining is used for mining steep deposits. Using this technique, mining first occurs at

PERSPECTIVES

WORKING UNDERGROUND

The deepest continuous mine shaft in the United States goes 7,000 feet (2,134 m) under the surface. Working this far underground can be dangerous. Miners are at risk of becoming trapped or crushed in a mine collapse. They also work with explosives that can put them in danger. But some miners enjoy the unique experience of their jobs. Curtis Burton has worked in underground mines for 17 years. He said, "Every day when you go underground you're seeing a part of the earth nobody else is seeing ever. I always thought it was neat."

the bottom of the mine and then works its way to the top. Tunnels are made at various depths. The lowest tunnel may be at the base of the deposit. Chutes and loading sites branch out from the tunnels. Explosives are placed in the floor of the second-lowest tunnel. The blast breaks up the material that lies between the two lowest tunnels. The broken rock and ore take up more space than they did before the blast. The material begins to fill the chutes and loading sites at the bottom of the mine. It can then be loaded into vehicles and taken to the surface.

An underground mine typically has multiple shrinkage stope mining sites. Several tunnels run under the bottom of the deposit. Walls are left between the tunnels. The overburden above the tunnels is mined first. After all the ore has been extracted in the tunnels, miners can go back and mine the walls for more materials.

Shrinkage stope mining creates an empty space underground. This space can be filled with waste rock. The waste rock fills the space to the level of what had been the second-lowest layer of the mine. This layer now becomes the bottom of the mine, and shrinkage stope mining continues. This technique of refilling the empty space is called cut-and-fill stoping.

Block caving is another mining technique where materials are extracted from the bottom of a mine. This technique is used when there are large ore bodies

HOW SHRINKAGE STOPE MINING WORKS

Shrinkage stope mining is an underground mining technique. Primary stopes are mined first. Then secondary stopes, the pillars between primary stopes, are mined. Blasting at the top of a stope causes ore to fall to the level below. How does this diagram help you understand this mining technique? Why is it necessary to plan ahead when developing a mine?

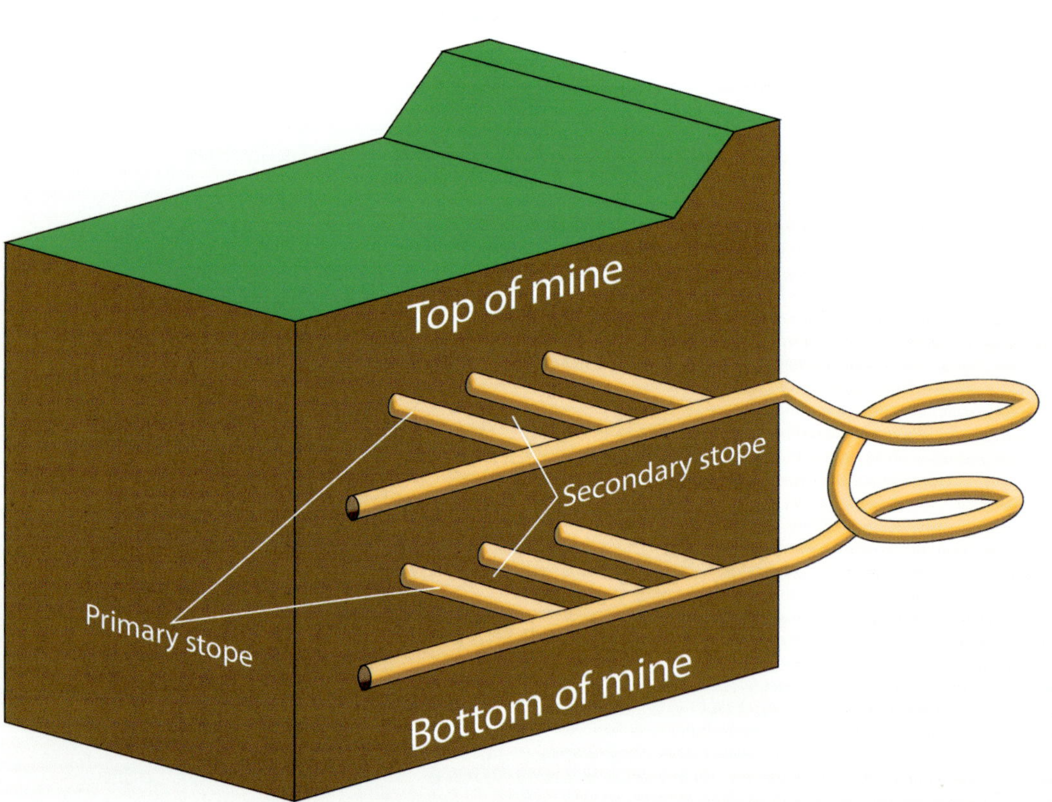

of low-grade materials that extend deep underground. Low-grade materials are less pure and less valuable than high-grade materials. A grid of tunnels is made at the bottom of the ore deposit. Another grid is made above the bottom grid. The two grids are connected by a series of funnels, which allow blasted material to fall into loading sites. The materials are crushed and brought to the surface through shafts. As materials are extracted from the mine, the area around the surface of the mine begins to sink.

FURTHER EVIDENCE

Chapter Three describes several underground mining techniques. What was one of the main points of this chapter? What evidence is included to support this point? Read the article at the website below. Does the information on the website support the main point of the chapter? Does it present new evidence?

UNDERGROUND MINING

abdocorelibrary.com/mining-techniques

tmc

UNDERWATER MINING

Underwater mining is used to access deposits in coastal waters, the seabed, and the ocean. Different mining techniques are necessary depending on water depth. Technology exists for mining in shallow waters. However, mining in the deep ocean is still experimental.

There are challenges with underwater mining. Seabed and deep-sea mining are affected by water pressure. Water pressure increases as a person or machine goes deeper

Scientists return to shore after doing research on how deep-sea mining may affect ocean health.

in the sea or ocean. Underwater mining equipment must be able to withstand this extreme pressure. In addition, there must be an efficient way to bring the mined material to the surface. New technologies will need to be developed so that equipment can be operated remotely. This means people will be able to control the equipment without going underwater themselves.

DREDGING

While technologies to mine deep underwater are still being developed, mining companies have established several techniques that can be used to mine in shallow water. These are dredging techniques. Dredging is used to mine materials such as gravel, sand, and rock. Gold can also be mined in shallow water. Dredging can occur at the bottom of rivers and lakes.

A dredge is a boat that is used to extract materials from underwater. There are several ways it does this. Some dredges have a chain of buckets that can be lowered underwater. The buckets scoop up

In the United States, a permit is needed to dispose of uncontaminated dredged materials into the ocean.

materials from the bottom and bring them back to the surface. Other dredges have a single large claw that grabs materials.

Dredges may also bring materials to the surface using a suction hose. This hose works similarly to a vacuum cleaner. It sucks materials from the bottom of the water. This technique is most effective at extracting lightweight materials from shallow waters. A very strong vacuum is needed to lift heavy materials

DEEP-SEA MINING SHIP OR SPY SHIP?

The construction of the *Glomar Explorer* submarine was funded by billionaire Howard Hughes and completed in 1974. Hughes's company stated that the ship was built to mine manganese nodules from the ocean floor. But it was actually constructed to recover the Soviet submarine K-129, which had sunk northwest of Hawaii in 1968. The *Glomar* managed to recover part of the submarine before a newspaper broke the story that it was part of a US government mission and not intended for mining. It would be more than 30 years before actual mining of the nodules was in the planning stage.

over a long distance. Dredging techniques provide the basis for deep-sea mining.

SEABED AND DEEP-SEA MINING

Seabed and deep-sea mining both occur on the ocean floor. Seabed mining typically occurs close to the coast. The deepest seabed mines are about 656 feet (200 m) below the surface of the water. Seabed mining uses many dredging techniques.

Suction is the most effective extraction technique at that depth.

Mining that goes deeper than 656 feet (200 m) is called deep-sea mining. Deep-sea mining is of high interest to mining companies. The demand for metals and minerals grows each year. Many of the minerals found on the deep ocean's floor are used today to produce electronics and batteries. These minerals include copper, cobalt, nickel, manganese, lead, lithium, titanium, platinum, gold, and zinc. Mining companies are interested in collecting polymetallic nodules from the ocean floor. These nodules contain many valuable metals, including nickel and cobalt.

Because polymetallic nodules lie on top of the ocean floor, collection of these nodules does not require drilling. Deep-sea mining techniques are still under development. One possible way to collect these nodules is to use a remotely operated vehicle. This vehicle would be lowered to the bottom of the ocean from a ship. It would then drive along the ocean floor

Metals such as manganese and cobalt can be found in polymetallic nodules, *pictured*. These metals are necessary for developing devices that can store renewable energy.

and scoop up nodules. The vehicle would be connected to the ship by a suction hose that pumps the nodules out of the water. Another hose or pipe would extend back into the ocean. It would return unwanted materials to the ocean floor.

Other resources lie beneath the ocean floor. Drilling would be necessary to access deep-sea deposits of minerals such as sulfide and manganese. Once loosened, these materials would be sucked up to the surface through a pipe. Unwanted materials would be sorted out and dumped back into the sea.

As of late 2022, deep-sea mining was illegal in international waters. Deep-sea mining disturbs the ocean floor habitat. It could also affect the sea life that lives in the deep ocean. Scientists are concerned that the unwanted materials released in the ocean could contain toxic metals that would contaminate the water. A few mining companies have been allowed to explore and test deep-sea mining techniques. They are

PERSPECTIVES

OCEAN HEALTH

Many marine scientists are concerned that deep-sea mining would affect ocean health. Water pressure and other factors make the deep ocean difficult to explore. Much of the wildlife in the ocean is still undiscovered. These scientists want more research to be done before deep-sea mining starts. They want to be sure that the risks of this type of mining are well understood. Jeff Drazen is a marine biologist. He spoke of his concerns about deep-sea mining. "I generally don't think it's possible for us to objectively assess all the risks involved right now," he said. "This is the poorest-described ecosystem on the planet."

This artwork shows how deep-sea mining may look in the future.

searching for ways to mine the valuable deposits without harming the environment.

Deep-sea mining techniques are still being developed. But many other techniques have been created for surface, underground, and underwater mines. These techniques are necessary to extract materials as safely and efficiently as possible. Mining is a major part of the US economy. Efficient mining techniques are necessary to produce the materials that people need for energy, transportation, and everyday objects.

STRAIGHT TO THE SOURCE

Gerard Barron is the chief executive officer of The Metals Company, a deep-sea mining company formerly known as DeepGreen Metals. In an interview, Barron responded to a question about the effect of deep-sea mining on the seafloor.

> *The seafloor is not pristine. It's heavily impacted by what we do on land, whether it's burning fossil fuels or polluting rivers with plastic that ends up in our oceans, or deep-sea [mining waste]. . . . We don't fully understand what the impact of getting all these metals is, but we are aware of the impact of destroying biodiverse ecosystems [from land mining] and dumping the waste in the ocean.*

Source: Robin Hicks. "We Need to Mine Deep-Sea Metals to Power the Energy Transition: DeepGreen CEO Gerard Barron." *Eco-Business*, 22 Oct. 2020, eco-business.com. Accessed 13 Oct. 2022.

WHAT'S THE BIG IDEA?

Read the primary text carefully and determine its main idea. Explain how the main idea is supported by details, naming two or three of those details.

FAST FACTS

- Mining companies employ mineral explorers and mine planners. They help mining companies find new mining sites and determine which mining technique would be best for a site.
- Surface mining is used when the deposits are near the surface. Open-pit, strip, highwall, and mountaintop removal techniques are used for surface mining.
- Surface mines are cheaper to develop than underground mines. Underground mines require more workers. They also have to meet more safety measures to ensure workers are safe.
- Room and pillar mining is used in underground mines when deposits are level and deep underground. Mining companies can increase the production of room and pillar mining by using retreat mining and longwall mining.
- Shrinkage stope mining and block caving are two underground mining techniques that can be used when the conditions of a deposit are not suitable for room and pillar mining.

- Dredging is an underwater mining technique. Buckets or a suction hose can be used to extract materials from the bottom of shallow bodies of water.
- Research is being done to explore the possibility of deep-sea mining. Valuable metals can be found on the ocean floor.
- Scientists want more research on the environmental effects of deep-sea mining before it is permitted.

STOP AND THINK

Tell the Tale

Chapter One of this book describes the operations of the Bingham Canyon mine. Pretend you are a miner working there. Write 200 words about your experience. Do you think you would like to be a miner? Why or why not?

Surprise Me

Chapter Two of this book talks about surface mining. After reading this book, what two or three facts about this kind of mining did you find the most surprising? Write a few sentences about each fact. Why did you find each fact surprising?

Take a Stand

Scientists argue that underwater mining may damage the environment. They say that underwater mining should not be allowed until more research is done. Mining companies say that the minerals on the ocean floor are necessary to make new products. Which viewpoint do you agree with? Why?

Why Do I Care?

Maybe you do not know anyone who works in a mine. But that doesn't mean you can't think about the importance of planning for the development of a new mine. Why is it important to investigate deposits before establishing a mine? How does careful planning affect costs? How does it affect the safety of miners?

GLOSSARY

assess
to look carefully at something and estimate its value or usefulness

contaminate
to make impure or unclean

emissions
substances released into the air, especially harmful gases

excavate
to dig out and remove, often forming a cavity

extract
to remove a mineral or metal from rock

mineral
a naturally occurring material that is typically found underground

nodule
a small, rounded lump of a mineral

profitable
able to make money

shaft
a vertical tunnel used to mine materials underground

solution
a liquid in which something has been dissolved

toxic
dangerous or poisonous

ONLINE RESOURCES

To learn more about mining techniques, visit our free resource websites below.

Visit **abdocorelibrary.com** or scan this QR code for free Common Core resources for teachers and students, including vetted activities, multimedia, and booklinks, for deeper subject comprehension.

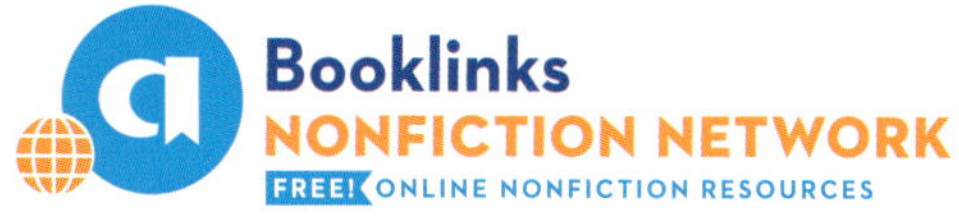

Visit **abdobooklinks.com** or scan this QR code for free additional online weblinks for further learning. These links are routinely monitored and updated to provide the most current information available.

LEARN MORE

Daly, Ruth. *How We Use Rocks and Minerals*. Crabtree, 2021.

Gagne, Tammy. *Mineral Processing*. Abdo, 2024.

Lusted, Marcia Amidon. *Fossils, Rocks, and Minerals*. Abdo, 2022.

INDEX

About the Author

Bonnie Hinman lives in southwestern Missouri with her husband, Bill, near her children and grandchildren. Lead and zinc mining was done within a few miles of her home before the area was mined out in the mid-1900s. Hinman has written more than 65 nonfiction books.